D1244332

EXTREME WINTER
SPORTS ZONE

SKI SLOPESTYLE

Darice Bailer

Lerner Publications Company • Minneapolis

Lerner Publications Company
A division of Lerner Publishing Group, Inc.
241 First Avenue North
Minneapolis, MN 55401 U.S.A.

Website address: www.lernerbooks.com

Content Consultant: Skogen Sprang, Freeskiing pioneer, X Games medalist, and current U.S. Freeskiing Slopestyle Team coach

With special thanks to Justine Spence, the U.S. Freeskiing press officer, freeskiing pioneer Mike Douglas, and skier Keri Herman for all of their help

Library of Congress Cataloging-in-Publication Data
Bailer, Darice.
    Ski slopestyle / by Darice Bailer.
        pages   cm. — (Extreme winter sports zone)
    Includes index.
    ISBN 978-1-4677-0756-5 (lib. bdg. : alk. paper)
    ISBN 978-1-4677-1731-1 (eBook)
    1. Skis and skiing—Juvenile literature. I. Title.
    GV854.315.B35 2014
    796.93—dc23   2012048749

Manufactured in the United States of America
1 – PP – 7/15/13

The images in this book are used with the permission of: © Aaron Ontiveroz/The Denver Post/ AP Images, 5, 6; © Robert Fullerton/Shutterstock Images, 7; © Beelde Photography/Shutterstock Images, 8, 13, 19, 27, 28 (top); © AP Images, 9; © Jim Cole/AP Images, 10; © Shutterstock Images, 11, 12; © Doug Pensinger/Getty Images, 14; © Alessandro Trovati/AP Images, 15; © Hannah Johnston/Getty Images, 16; © Nathan Bilow/AP Images, 17, 18, 25; © ARENA Creative/ iStockphoto, 20; © Jeff McIntosh/AP Images, 21; © Irina Rogova/Shutterstock Images, 22; © Ben Haslam/Haslam Photography/Shutterstock Images, 22–23, 29 (bottom); © Volodymyr Krasyuk/ Shutterstock Images, 23; © Chris Fryer/The Saginaw News/AP Images, 24; © Jean-Pierre Clatot/ AFP/Getty Images, 26; © Daniel Petty/The Denver Post/AP Images, 28 (bottom); © Mark J. Terrill/ AP Images, 29 (top).

Front cover: © Marcel Jancovic/Shutterstock.com; backgrounds: © kcv/Shutterstock.com.

Main body text set in Folio Std Light 11/17.
Typeface provided by Adobe Systems.

TABLE OF CONTENTS

CHAPTER ONE

LET'S GO SHRED! (LET'S SKI!)

It was January 26, 2012. American skier Tom Wallisch shot down the wintry Colorado slope. It was his final run at ESPN's Winter X Games. Wallisch was 24 years old. He was going for a gold medal in ski slopestyle.

Ski slopestyle combines traditional downhill skiing with spins, flips, and other amazing acrobatics. Athletes ski down a course covered with man-made features like kickers (snowy jumps), rails, and boxes (wider rails). Skiers perform as many difficult tricks as they can. But they try to keep their tricks and landings stylish and smooth.

THE X GAMES

ESPN has held the X Games, a competition for extreme sports, since 1995. At first the X Games featured summer sports such as skateboarding and inline skating. Then, in 1997, ESPN launched the Winter X Games. Men's ski slopestyle appeared for the first time in 2002. Women's ski slopestyle was added seven years later. The Winter X Games are held twice a year, in Aspen, Colorado, and Tignes, France. Skiers compete for gold, silver, and bronze medals. Athletes also earn prize money.

Tom Wallisch proved he was one of the best slopestyle skiers in the world when he competed at the 2012 Winter X Games in Aspen, Colorado.

Even though he was the youngest athlete competing in the event, Nick Goepper came close to winning the gold medal in ski slopestyle at the 2012 Winter X Games. He walked away with a silver medal.

Wallisch the Magician

Wallisch made skiing look easy. One announcer called Wallisch a magician. He had pulled off unbelievable stunts in the air. However, a 17-year-old rookie named Nick Goepper was in the lead in the final run. Wallisch would need to perform some spectacular tricks to grab the lead back and win.

That night, Wallisch hopped onto a box. Then he leaped onto a rail, sliding 25 feet (7.6 meters). He spun around and landed. But he saved his most dangerous trick for last. Wallisch skied up the jump backward and turned upside down in the air. He reached back to grab one of his skis. Then he spun like a corkscrew three full times. He soared higher and higher. Finally, Wallisch landed. His landing was smooth. It was as if he had never left the ground.

At the bottom of the hill, Wallisch smiled and waited for his score. After a few seconds, the judges announced it. Wallisch's score was a 96 out of 100. Almost perfect! Wallisch won the gold medal. He also earned the highest score in ski slopestyle history.

Wallisch set a new record high score with his awesome Winter X Games run in 2012.

CHAPTER TWO

TWIN-TIPS AND HISTORY

Slopestyle skiers, such as Tae Westcott, do exciting tricks on ski slopes.

Slopestyle skiing is actually part of a style of skiing called freeskiing. Freeskiing is a type of downhill skiing where skiers can do incredible tricks. Their skiing style is more like snowboarding than regular downhill skiing.

Freestyle Is Born

Freeskiing is a fairly new sport. But its roots go back a long way. In the 1920s, American skiers began flipping and spinning down ski courses. This style of skiing was called freestyle. Bumps called moguls were soon added to the courses. Mogul skiing officially became part of the Winter Olympic Games in 1992. In 1994 jumps called kickers were added to Olympic courses. Kickers are used in aerial tricks.

Fourteen-year-old Andrea Mead Lawrence was a part of the U.S. Women's Downhill Ski Team in 1948.

Some skiers couldn't get enough of this new take on their sport. They did even wilder tricks than most freestyle skiers. Freeskiing grew out of this revolution. These daring athletes were inspired by snowboard moves and tried crazy tricks on skis. Some freeskiers even took their skis to snowboard parks. This was the birth of ski slopestyle.

AN ANCIENT SPORT

Skiing first appeared in the Olympic Games in 1924. But the sport has been around much longer. Humans have been skiing down hills and mountains for thousands of years. The oldest skis were found in Russia and are more than 7,000 years old! They were probably made before the invention of the wheel. Up until around 1900, skis were mostly used for hunting, transportation, and delivering mail. Now people use them for fun!

Terrain parks, such as this one in New Hampshire, provide features that snowboarders can use to do tricks.

Skogen Sprang was one of the first kids to take up slopestyle. In the late 1990s, when Sprang was a teenager, terrain parks began opening across the United States. These were snowy playgrounds for snowboarders. Terrain parks had rails, ramps called half-pipes, and other features people used for tricks. But skiers were not allowed at the terrain parks. So Sprang and other skiers sneaked into the parks to ski the slopes.

Getting into the parks wasn't the only problem. Traditional skis weren't shaped like snowboards. Skis curled up in front but not in back. This shape didn't allow skiers to ski backward. Sprang needed a ski that allowed him to land a jump backward. Lucky for Sprang, a coach named Mike Douglas was looking for the same thing.

FREESTYLE FIRSTS

- **1924:** The first Winter Olympic Games are held in the French Alps in Chamonix, France.
- **1988:** Freestyle skiing is first demonstrated at the Calgary Olympic Games.
- **1992:** Mogul skiing becomes an Olympic sport.
- **1994:** Aerial skiing becomes an Olympic sport.
- **2010:** Ski cross (ski racing) is added to the Olympic Games.
- **2011:** Two freeskiing events, ski half-pipe and ski slopestyle, are added to the 2014 Olympic Games.

Traditional skis curl up in the front but not in the back. This design makes it hard for skiers to land backward.

A New Ski

Douglas was a skier who helped coach the Canadian National Mogul Team. On his days off, Douglas liked to visit a snowboarding park. Snowboarders copied skateboard moves in the snow. Douglas liked their moves. He wanted to try some of their tricks on skis. But, like Sprang, he had trouble landing backward. In the spring of 1997, Douglas had an idea. What if he designed a new ski that curled up on both ends? Then skiers could land in any direction. It would be a twin-tip ski. Douglas drew up a proposal for this new ski. He sent this proposal to some ski manufacturers. A ski company called Salomon thought it was a great idea. The company soon began making a twin-tip ski called the Salomon Teneighty.

Pioneers of freeskiing tried to land snowboarding tricks on their skis.

Twin-tip skis allow skiers to both land and ski backward.

The Teneighty was the first of its kind. Its tips were more flexible. This meant skiers could push off more easily and land backward. As for the name, a full-circle spin is a 360. Skiers hoped that one day, they would use the Teneighty to spin around three complete times in the air. This would be a 1080.

The first U.S. Freeskiing Open competition was held in Vail, Colorado, in 1998 with the new Teneighty skis. Freeskiing was on! And Skogen Sprang, the teenager who used to sneak into snowboard parks, would grow up to become a professional skier. Eventually he became the coach of the U.S. Freeskiing Slopestyle Pro Team.

Pushing the Sport

Men's ski slopestyle first appeared at the Winter X Games in 2002. But it took several years before women could compete. Canadian skier Sarah Burke helped make that happen. When slopestyle was first added to the Winter X Games, there weren't enough women for a separate competition. Burke wanted to compete with the guys. But contest organizers wouldn't allow it.

Burke hounded the X Games. Did they have any girls yet? Finally, because of Burke's pushing, women's slopestyle became part of the Winter X Games in 2009. During those games, Burke became the first woman to land a

Sarah Burke pressured the X Games to let women compete in ski slopestyle. Burke took seventh place in the women's slopestyle competition at the Winter X Games in 2009.

1080 in a competition. She spun around three full times before landing. Burke competed in slopestyle and superpipe, an event where skiers do tricks off a giant half-pipe ramp. Burke loved freeskiing and fought hard for the sport to be included in the Olympic Games. The International Olympic Committee noticed how popular slopestyle skiing was becoming. The committee added the sport to the 2014 Olympic Games.

Construction on the athletes' village began early for the 2014 Winter Olympic Games in Sochi, Russia.

CHAPTER THREE

SKIING TO WIN

Slopestyle skiers love their sport. Competitions around the world bring these athletes together. The competitions give slopestyle skiers a chance to compete against one another.

Slopestyle Competitions

Juniors are the fastest-growing group of freeskiers. Each year young freeskiers have the chance to participate in the Junior Freeride Tour. The tour is open to boys and girls between the ages of 12 and 18.

Pros also face off at major ski competitions. They compete at events such as the International Ski Federation World Cup and

Bobby Brown (center), Gus Kenworthy (left), and Jonas Hunziker (right) earned the gold, silver, and bronze medals, respectively, at the 2010 Snowboard Junior World and Freestyle Championships.

Grete Eliassen went home with a silver medal after the women's ski slopestyle competition at the 2009 Winter X Games.

Mountain Dew's Dew Tour. The Winter and European X Games have two of the biggest ski slopestyle competitions.

Skiers who win major competitions can earn a spot on the U.S. Freeskiing Slopestyle Team. The professional team usually has 10 skiers on the team—five men and five women. These skiers train together and travel all over the world.

SLOPESTYLE SAFETY

Ski slopestyle is exciting, but it can also be very dangerous. Pros and amateurs can get seriously injured or even killed in a bad fall. Slopestyle skiers should always wear a helmet, goggles, and protective pads. But even when wearing protective gear, skiers can still get hurt. Beginners should take lessons from an experienced skier. All slopestyle skiers should try tricks only within their abilities.

BUILDING A SLOPESTYLE COURSE

What does it take to build a ski slopestyle course? Lots of planning and months of work. It took more than 2,600 hours to build the ski, snowboard, and snowmobile courses at the 2012 Winter X Games. Athletes and course builders first laid out designs. Then they carved the course out of the base of Buttermilk Mountain in Colorado. The course included four jumps and two rails.

On the Course

One of the coolest parts about ski slopestyle is that skiers can compete in snow all year round. While it's summer in the northern half of the hemisphere, it's winter in the southern half.

Every course is different, and skiers don't know what to expect. Course designers can create whatever rails and jumps they want. Men and women ski down the same course, which is about 2,132 to 2,296 feet (650 to 700 m) long. That's a little less than half a mile (0.8 kilometers).

Skiers practice on new slopestyle courses to learn where the jumps, rails, and other features are located.

All slopestyle skiers have an individual style that sets them apart from their competitors.

Skiers can choose which stunts they want to do. They're judged on the number, difficulty, and performance of their tricks. Performance includes the landing and smoothness of their run. They're also judged on amplitude (how high they jump) and style.

Ski slopestyle can be a tough sport to judge. Skiers have their own styles. These styles can be very different from one another. Fortunately, many judges are former slopestyle skiers who know the sport very well.

SKI SPEAK
Dub: a double flip
Sick: something amazing

CHAPTER FOUR

HIT THE RAILS

Slopestyle may be a young sport, but already it's attracting millions of skiers. Many ski resorts are trying to draw rookie jibbers. These resorts build entry-level parks with small jumps or features. The resorts also offer programs to teach kids how to ski.

Where to Shred

Freestyle America runs many programs for kids at ski locations. The organization offers camps so young skiers can safely develop their tricks. Some rookie skiers practice new tricks on trampolines. This helps them get comfortable doing somersaults in the air.

Kids can practice slopestyle skiing at many ski resorts.

Many freestyle skiers practice during the summer by jumping onto air bags.

Whistler Blackcomb Ski Resort in British Columbia offers spring, summer, fall, and winter camps for freestyle skiing. Campers can ski up a snowy jump and land on a huge air bag. The air bag is a giant inflatable cushion that helps skiers practice tricks without landing on the hard ground.

PROFESSIONAL PRACTICE

The U.S. Freeskiing Slopestyle Team practices tricks on trampolines and air bags. In the summer of 2012, the team trained at Windells in Sandy, Oregon, while preparing for the first World Cup Slopestyle. The skiers trained safely using air bags and the soft summer snow. The U.S. Ski and Snowboard Association also has a huge training center in Park City, Utah, called the Center of Excellence. The center has trampolines and a foam pit where the team can land tricks safely.

LOOKING STEEZY (STYLISH) WITH THE RIGHT EQUIPMENT

SKIS

A trained salesperson at a local ski shop or ski resort can help a skier find just the right twin-tips. Skis should usually come up to about a skier's nose.

BOOTS

Boots act like a skier's steering wheels. They are important for control. Boots cushion a landing too. A slopestyle skier's boots should fit nice and snug.

HELMET

A good helmet wraps snugly around the head to protect it in a hard fall. Beginners and pros alike need a special ski helmet with hard plastic. A bicycle helmet won't do.

GOGGLES

Goggles block out the sun's harmful rays and protect a skier's eyes from wind and snow. Shatterproof lenses will stay in one piece after a hard fall.

PADS

Forearm or elbow pads help cushion a skier's fall. Pads that go on a skier's back or padded shorts can help protect a skier's tailbone and hips.

Slopestyle skier Keri Herman wears all the right gear at a 2010 Dew Tour competition.

Both freeskiers and snowboarders can enjoy the features of terrain parks.

The Courses

Terrain parks have several jumps, rails, and flat boxes (long, thin boxes). These features are fun to hit (do tricks off). But an athlete needs good form. Hips should be lined up over the feet, and skiers should keep their heads up and stay alert.

Terrain parks can be fun but dangerous. Slopestyle skiers should check out a feature before using it. They need to make sure it's safe and clear of other riders. Then skiers warn other riders to wait their turn. Most skiers raise a ski pole or a hand and call, "Dropping in!"

Flat-Box Skiing

A flat box is one of the easiest features to ski. A skier should approach the flat box with ski tips pointed straight ahead. Then the skier can hop on the box. Skiers should stay balanced while on the flat box. At the end, skiers jump off. They should bend their knees to cushion their landings.

A 180-degree spin on a flat box is a gnarly trick. In a 180, a skier spins halfway around. Then the skier lands facing the opposite direction. To start, a skier should slowly approach the box. Then the skier hops on the box while spinning to face the other direction. The skier should keep looking over the shoulder to spot a good landing. Then the skier lands facing backward. Skiing backward is called switch skiing.

Sarah Burke rides a flat box at the 2009 Winter X Games.

Slopestyle skier Kaya Turski hits a rail at the 2012 European Winter X Games.

Rail Skiing

Rails are usually just 3 inches (7.6 centimeters) wide. Their narrow width makes them tricky. But beginners can do a basic rail slide. They should start by skiing toward the rail, then jumping on. Their boots should land centered on the rail. Then skiers can ride the rail sideways. Their boots and skis should be shoulder width apart. Once across the rail, the skiers can jump off facing forward.

Jumps

A little roller is a small jump that looks like a mound of snow. This is an easy jump for rookie slopestyle skiers. A skier should slowly approach the roller. Legs should be bent, and skis should be up. Then the skier can lean slightly back and fly! A roller is a good place to practice a 180. To do a switch-up on the roller, a skier should wait until boot heels are at the lip (tip) of the mound before spinning off.

Cool Moves

Grabbing a ski while jumping off a box or rail adds a little more style. Skiers raise the feet toward the chest for balance. Then they reach and grab a ski while flying through the air.

For a tuck or safety grab, skiers bring their feet up and then grab the right skis with their right hands or the left skis with their left hands. A skier should grab the outside edge of the ski under the boot.

In a trick called Japan, a skier grabs the inside of the ski behind the boot with the opposite hand. But the skier shouldn't forget to let go and should look for a good place to land.

People who pushed themselves to perform once-unimaginable moves created this sport. The doors are wide open for the next skiers to do the same with their own gnarly tricks!

SLOPESTYLE STARS

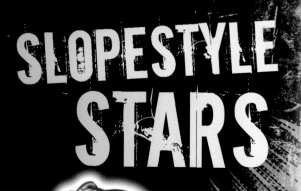

GUS KENWORTHY

Career highlights: Gus Kenworthy grew up in Telluride, Colorado. He started skiing in 1993 and is one of the best freeskiers around. He is a master of many types of freeskiing. Kenworthy won the Association of Freeskiing Professionals (AFP) Overall World Champion title in 2011 and 2012. That means he was the best in three freeskiing events: slopestyle, half-pipe, and big air.

BOBBY BROWN

Career highlights: In the winter of 2002–03, when he was 12 years old, U.S. skier Bobby Brown landed a 360 (one full spin) and his first backflip. He polished off the season with a 720 (two spins). The next year, Brown landed a switch 900 (two and a half spins). Brown still has some of the best slopestyle tricks around. He may do a triple cork, where his head goes below his feet three times. He can even flip four times in the air before landing.

KERI HERMAN

Career highlights: Keri Herman grew up playing ice hockey in Minnesota. She started skiing in 2004 after moving to Colorado for college. The rest was history. Herman is a member of the U.S. Freeskiing Slopestyle Team. In 2012 Herman was number 3 on the AFP's Women's Overall World Ranking list.

KAYA TURSKI

Career highlights: Most fans agree that Canadian skier Kaya Turski is one of the best female slopestyle skiers. In March 2011, Turski became the first woman to land a switch 1080 (three spins). In 2012 Turski became the first woman to win three gold medals in a row at the Winter X Games for ski slopestyle.

GLOSSARY

ACROBATICS

gymnastic-like stunts

AERIAL

in the air

AMATEUR

someone who participates in an activity for fun without expectation of payment

AMPLITUDE

the height a skier soars during a trick

FREESKIING

a type of skiing that combines skiing with flips, twists, and other tricks

HALF-PIPE

a snowy ramp that looks like half the inside of a pipe

PROFESSIONAL

someone who participates in an activity as a job for payment

ROLLER

a small snowy hill

ROOKIE

someone who is new to a sport or an activity

SWITCH

skiing backward

FOR MORE INFORMATION

Further Reading

Bailer, Darice. *Ski Superpipe*. Minneapolis: Lerner Publications, 2014.

Kelley, K. C. *Freestyle Skiing*. Mankato, MN: Child's World, 2011.

MacAulay, Kelley, and Bobbie Kalman. *Extreme Skiing*. New York: Crabtree, 2006.

Websites

Association of Freeskiing Professionals
http://afpworldtour.com/afp10/
The official website for the Association of Freeskiing Professionals has information on the AFP World Tour. Check out the latest news and rankings.

The Olympic Games
http://www.olympic.org/
The official home of the Olympic Games with a history of freestyle skiing and a link to the International Ski Federation website.

U.S. Freeskiing Teams
http://usfreeskiing.com/freeskiing
Read the latest news about the U.S. freeskiing teams as they prepare for the next Olympic Games.

INDEX

About the Author

Darice Bailer has written many books for children. She won the Parents' Choice Gold Award for her first book, *Puffin's Homecoming*. She began her career as a sports reporter and is especially fond of writing about sports for kids. She lives in Connecticut with her husband.